Norman Schwenk's new collection, *Book of Songs*, brings together poems and song lyrics of many varieties: love songs and ballads, dance and battle songs; satires and laments; there is a march, a lullaby, a hymn, a rock-and-roll song, a Christmas carol, a birthday song, a cowboy song, and even a song for a klezmer band.

His models are the Scots bard Robbie Burns and the Essex singer-songwriter Adrian May, whom he calls his 'song-writing mentor'. He also pays homage to his American contemporary, Tom Waits, the Elizabethan song-writer, Thomas Campion, and the Victorian lyricist, W.S. Gilbert, whom he describes as 'an honorary Schwenk'.

Norman Schwenk was born and grew up in Nebraska and was educated in the USA. He taught literature and writing at the University of Pennsylvania, Uppsala University in Sweden and Cardiff University in Wales. Norman has been writing and publishing verse in the US and UK for more than 60 years. His most recent collections are: *The More Deceived: poems about love and lovers* (2005) and *Cadillac Temple: haiku sequences* (2010). Married to the Welsh writer Deborah Kay Davies, he lives in Cardiff.

'...a stimulating read...they richly reward rereading...fresh, vibrant, insightful...'

Nigel Jenkins on *Cadillac Temple*

'Norman Schwenk is a wordsmith of great quality, someone who can fix a moment or an idea and make it come alive on the page, taking the reader to places he never dreamed of going.'

Phil ⌐   1

YET AGAIN, WITH LOVE, FOR DEBORAH

Book of Songs

Norman Schwenk

Parthian, Cardigan SA43 1ED
www.parthianbooks.com
© Norman Schwenk 2015
ISBN 978-1-910409-87-9
Cover by Richard Cox
Typeset by Elaine Sharples
Printed and bound by Gomer Press, Llandysul
Published with the financial support of the Welsh Books Council.
British Library Cataloguing in Publication Data
A cataloguing record for this book is available from the British Library.

Contents

A Morning Song

CHORUS: Good morning! *Coraggio*!
Don't be mad or blue
Remember almost everybody
Feels as bad as you
But the sun goes right on shining
When it's stuck behind a cloud
And the birds go right on singing
Though they're awful fucking loud

I knew a man from New York
Who thought he was betrayed
Whose brother requisitioned
All the money he had made
And did a flit to Florida
And on down to Brazil
And left him with a lawyer
And a bag of unpaid bills

He went to see his mistress
To renovate his pride
To say though she was on her own
He'd love her till he died
But there pinned on her pillow
Was a note that made him ill
It said, 'Gone with an old friend
On a trip down to Brazil'

He went home to the wife and kids
To get away from guile
To tell the wife they'd start again
And take it with a smile
But she told him, 'You can start again
Go ride your hobbyhorse
I'm going down to Rio
And I want a quick divorce'

He went to see his doctor
Feeling like an oily cheese
He learned he had contracted
An incurable disease
But the doctor said, 'Don't worry
Every day take ten of these
Though it may hurt in the morning
Live as long as you damn please'

Autumn Lullaby

Slumber, little stranger,
Child of family blood
Your mum and dad made you
Out of their own mud

Now you live among us
Sleeping in our care
You breathe the air
Drink the water
Eat the food we share

You give us back your laughter
Your listening, your noise
You lift us with your bravery
The glistening of your eyes

Sleep can be so easy
Pray the bugs won't bite
Then let the night
Fill your body
Till you see the light

Slumber, little stranger,
Child of family blood
Your mum and dad made you
Out of their own mud

A Woman For All Seasons (Foxtrot)

CHORUS: A Woman for All Seasons
                That's what I want to see
                I'll search until I find her
                And hope she fancies me

Crazy days of springtime
Summer with winter too
Once I had a girl like spring
So hot and cold she blew
You might suffer sunstroke
In the warmth of her embrace
And you could catch pneumonia
Simply standing in her space

Let-down months of summer
Promising all things nice
Once I had a girl like summer
Visions of paradise
Followed by disappointment
When her weather cast its spell
You never saw so much rain
Then it was hot as hell

MIDDLE EIGHT: I love every season
                      Mother Nature sends
                      It's what her daughters do with them
                      Drives me round the bend
                      Summer autumn winter spring
                      The planet's in a whirl
                      While I look for a lady
                      Who's an all-weather girl

Autumn is about dying
However lush the trees
Once I had a girl like autumn
Had me on my knees
Had me on my back as well
And standing on my head
So mixed up it's lucky
She didn't have me dead

Sombre days of winter
Unless you like the dark
Once I had a girl like winter
Nothing made her spark
Her Christmas lights were faulty
Her guiding star was blurred
She could wipe a sunny smile
With just a mouldy word

Birthday Song

O Frabjous Day, when you hove into view,
Our sweet treasure trove, we celebrate you;
Beats closing banks, giving thanks for the corn;
Our best holiday is the day you were born;
We celebrate saints, the year when it's new,
But the best, yes the best, is when it was you.

Blaspheming Hymn

Mary had a man
Joseph was his name
The Church denied his fatherhood
He was too old
She was too good
So Mary had the fame

Was it really fair
After he was dead
For gangs of priests to write him off
And say some high angelic toff
Kicked him out of bed?

Mary had a man
Three cheers for the dads
Who love their own and pay the bills
While gossips say somebody else
Fathered all the kids

Bobo Home

We have a cosy bobo home
Our rooms are full of junk
Our loft is rubbish to the roof
Won't take another trunk

We rent a storage cubicle
Where so much trash is piled
That when we try to get inside
It springs like something wild

We're sick of books that we won't read
Pictures that we won't see
Records we won't listen to
Old cups that leak your tea

We'll never wear these dated clothes
The shoes won't pinch our feet
This lamp will never light our way
The rugs we'll never beat

We'll never watch these DVDs
They'll never get to Oz
This chair will have no bottoms on
No flowers grace that vase

At least we'll feel at home again
When time has passed us by
We'll join that junkyard in the earth
Fly to that scrapyard in the sky

Carrickfergus

Blackthorn flowers
Now in Carrickfergus
The blackthorn flowers
Ghostly pale
And I dream of you
Spring in Carrickfergus
Whoever hears me
I tell your tale

I see you there
Autumn Carrickfergus
You pick the sloeberry
Black as night
I still see you there
Black against the heavens
The blackthorn branches
Holding you so tight

Lovely Christmas
We were lost in Heaven
We drank our sloeberry
Gin and wine
And we laughed and cried
Winter Carrickfergus
Where nights are long
By your lover's side

Come Eastertide
And the deathly flowers
Men good and true
Took her from my side
And they walled her in

Spring in Carrickfergus
Where stones are chilling
Where she paled and died

You fear woman
Men of Carrickfergus
You fear the she-devil
Casts her spell
Brews a witch's brew
For your sons and daughters
For Satan's trophies
In the halls of Hell

Men good and true
Men of Carrickfergus
Come Judgement Day
When we sinners rise
You will see the sloe
That forbidden berry
Bitter night-black berry
In your very eyes

Blackthorn flowers
Home in Carrickfergus
The blackthorn flowers
Deathly pale
And I dream of you
Spring in Carrickfergus
Whoever hears me
I tell your tale

Cheshire Cat Moon

I want to give you something when I go
I want to leave a little something when I'm gone
Here it is Here I go Carry on

The sky is blue
The river green
The clouds are white as white can be
Lovers make love
Under a hedge
Instead of a bed like you and me

Cheshire Cat moon
Perfect and wise
She smiles in a cold starry sky
Follows them home
Shines in their street
Beams in their dreams and winks her eye

The walls are white
The tulips red
Blood red like the nails on her toes
He washes up
Vacuums the rugs
Tidies the books in tidy rows

The clouds are grey
He's gone away
The long trip you travel for free
He lives in her
The bluebells blue
The snowdrops white as white can be

11

Drinking Song

CHORUS: You got no Heaven to raise you up
            You got no Hell to fear
            So come on, sing, and have a cup
            And help a needy brother to the beer

We don't want any dirty cops
We don't want any crime
We want a peaceful cottage
With excitement all the time
We don't want governments coming along
And ordering us to sin
We don't want any wars at all
And we want the Good to win

We don't condone adultery
We don't reject affairs
We want to be the sultan
And the guy who really cares
We don't want any witch of a woman
Putting us in a trance
We want to keep our liberty
And we want to lose our pants

We don't want any steady work
We only want success
We want to yawn upon the beach
And make the world progress
We want to stay as white as a lily
Wallowing in the slop
The kindly generous happy guys
Who rise up to the top

Drowning Song

CHORUS: It takes a strong swimmer
To save somebody drowning
To bring them from the bottom of the sea
Your loving arms are strong
So say it won't be long
Before you reach my hand to rescue me

I saw you on the beach today
You didn't even look my way
Your mind was on a million other things
I tried to wave and catch your eye
You didn't even hear me cry
'Hey, baby, have you got my water wings?'

I bought you peanuts and a coke
I thought we'd sit and have a smoke
And things might be the way they used to be
But you ran off and shut me out
You didn't even hear me shout
'Hey, baby, come on back, the treat's on me!'

Who was that nerdy little rat
The one who gave your cheek a pat
And giggled when you chased him down the sand?
How could you fool around that way
When I was floundering in the bay?
Oh, baby, here I am, please take my hand!

I'm going down a second time
You may be guilty of a crime
You act as though I'm bathing in a tub
But I'm a desperate drowning man
Oh take my desperate drowning hand
Oh, baby, blub blub blub blub blub blub blub

Friendship, Maybe More
(Soulmates' Song)

REFRAIN: For evenings, friendship, maybe more
              Braintree, Cardiff, or Anywhere

Would like to meet
Genuine gent
With dancing feet
Essex or Gwent
Own house and car
Must be sincere
Likes to go far
Has sweet top gear

Would like to meet
Good sense of humour
Sixties, petite
Widowed by tumour
Romantic, prudent
Likes pubs and walks
Keen full-time student
School of Hard Knocks

BRIDGE:
He might be your Mr Wow
Battersea, Bristol or Penhow
She might be your Mrs Right
Ullapool or the Isle of Wight

WLTM
My kind of guy
Crème de la crème
Not crème de la pie
Likes dogs and kids
Bit of a Fagin
Like me N/S
Born-again Pagan

WLTM
Tropical cruises
Caring and warm
Loves wine and roses
Solvent and slim
Maybe too busty
Likes a good film
Wheelchair, but lusty

Growler And His Girl (Slow Waltz)

They meet in a bar
He asks her to dance
He knows a catalogue of steps
She dances alone
And watches him move
He's sweet and totally inept

He growls when he sings
She warbles and trills
They're not a Disney song at sunset
He wears a bowler hat
She goes the whole hog
A tweed pencil skirt, pearls and twin set

She drives to her job
He watches her go
Worried she'll be strawberry jam
He busses to work
Where he growls for coins
A one-man tin-pan-alley band

The night it is black
They're both wide awake
Telling one another their dreams
His dream is boring
Hers is appalling
Of Corgis servicing The Queen

They're slimming together
Eating pulses and leaves
No sugar, no saturates, no booze
It's like when they gamble
They're spinning, they're winning
Then shocked to discover they lose

It's one of those days
They're both feeling low
Feeling low and flat as the floor
Suddenly she farts
Pardon me, she says
And they're laughing, farting some more

They're watching TV
They shout at the screen
Accusing the government of crimes
Then brush their teeth
And climb the stairs
To bed where everything is fine

The Growler and his Girl
Lived a long time ago
They were not very good or bad
Not so very brave
Maybe not so wise
But they loved me, my Mum, my Dad

Hanging Song

I talked to a stone this morning
This stone he talked to me
He sighed inside my prison wall
And said these words to me

O I wish I was a man like you
As free as any king
You promenade all over the room
Do almost anything

You ought to be a stone like me
There's nothing I can do
I sit here without a hope in the world
Not even a change of view
Not even a change of view

I talked to a rat this morning
This rat he talked to me
He skittered across my prison floor
And said these words to me

O I wish I was a man like you
As lazy as a king
You lay around in bed all day
You don't do anything

You ought to be a rat like me
It's work the whole day long
Nobody ever gave me a thing
And what have I done wrong?
What have I done wrong?

I talked to a bird this morning
This bird he talked to me
He whistled behind my prison bars
And said these words to me

O I wish I was a man like you
As cosy as a king
You sit here without a worry in sight
As safe as anything

You ought to be a bird like me
It's danger all the time
I dodge the milliners, boys and cats
As though I'd committed a crime
As though I'd committed a crime

I talked to a rope this morning
This rope he talked to me
He groaned and looked me in the eye
And said these words to me

O I wish I was a man like you
A man's a happy king
When I throw my arms around their necks
They chuckle, dance and sing

You ought to be a rope like me
It's seldom any fun
There's nothing to do but hang around
And hope some party comes
Hope some party comes

Happy Tramper

It's peaceful out here by the bins
The lanes don't have people or cars
When my work is done
I sit in the sun
If it rains I can always go in

When it's cold there's exhaust from kitchens
Or the laundries hissing with steam
If you live in a house
You're snug as a louse
But you get fat and sit around bitchin'

There's nourishing things here to eat
You've got to stay healthy and trim
If you're a real tramper
You're strong as a dancer
Especially your legs and your feet

It's tramping that gives you the buzz
There's so many places to be
A walk can be hell
That doesn't go well
But it's heaven on earth if it does

It's peaceful out here by the bins
The lanes don't have people or cars
When my work is done
I sit in the sun
If it rains I can always crawl in

Homeless

A house is not a home without a loo
The workmen said they'd be a day or two
Now I haven't got a home
I'm a king without a throne
And my castle moat is full of one and two

A home is not a sofa and TV
The workmen said there'd be an extra fee
But you need a bath to be in
And you need a pot to pee in
What feels more fundamental than a wee?

A home is not a kitchen or a bed
They'd be another week the workmen said
But you won't smell like a flower
If you haven't had a shower
Your odour may resemble something dead

A house is not a home without a loo
The workmen say they don't know what to do
So I haven't got a home
I'm a king without a throne
And my moat's afloat with doo doody doo

House Of The Setting Sun (Torch Song)

CHORUS: No one goes out shopping
          No one's minding the shop
          Everyone buys in Neverland
          Everyone sells by sleight-of-hand
          Be bop   Doo wop   Doo wop

Our Christian Bookshop's shut
Where Jesus plied his trade
The self-same house where Mrs Foster
And her slightly cockeyed daughter
Thousands of times got laid

Jesus and Mrs Foster
They met you face to face
They knew you wanted books or sex
They let you look and touch low-tech
They charged you a fair price

Now everyone goes on line
It's Heaven if you're shy
People pretend to be your friend
No one winks or tweaks your nipple
Or looks you in the eye

Bless the soul of this house
Say goodbye to the real
Come meet the spooks of Cyberhell
Ring the bell—they answer the knell
And offer you a deal

Kiss The Devil (Battle Song)

CHORUS: If you kiss the Devil
Your breath smells of brimstone
The sulphur stink follows you around
You make a magic circle
Everybody backs away
When you kiss the Devil you go down

There was a lad from my town
Who vowed to beat the Devil
And be a mighty warrior for the Good
But when the Devil kissed him
He thought the arrow missed him
Only the Devil knew he was dead

The lad fought with courage
In the midst of the carnage
For he was fighting Evil hearts and hands
He killed without a pinch
Of regret—he didn't flinch
He didn't know he was the Devil's man

And who's to say he knew
When the Devil ran him through
Stabbed him in the back? Well it was war
He died a hero's death
With sulphur on his breath
He never knew he was the Devil's whore

Knots And Ties

When I was a little boy
I learned to tie my shoe
Make a pretty tidy bow
Pull it tight and off I'd go
Skipping up and down the stair
Safe as houses, unaware
I might be tripping on a lace
And falling on my stupid face

When I was a bigger boy
I learned to tie my tie
Windsor, four-in-hand or bow
Every knot there was to know
Neckties weren't for rain and storm
Didn't keep you dry or warm
I'd step out sleek and proud and vain
To show the world my gravy stain

When I was a youngish man
I tied the tie that binds
Worked so hard to knot it tight
Souls and bodies to unite
Sheepshank, granny, hangman's noose
Slip and square—they all came loose
Nobody suffered more than me
From D-I-V-O-R-C-E

When I was an older man
I tied myself in knots
Want, disease, injustice, war
Every cause worth fighting for
I fought to put the world to rights
But I'd get knotted every night
And while I struggled every day
The old world went its merry way

And now I am an old man
I've done with knots and ties
I'm free of all that binding stuff
Don't tie me down—I've had enough
It's velcro slip-ons for my feet
My turkey neck is bare as meat
One ready-knotted tie does fine
The black tie ready-stained with wine

Lonesome Cowboy

It's lonesome out here on the range
With only the cattle to sing to
No comfort by day, no wonder by night
And only my saddle to cling to

By day I see plains of brown grass
Whether rolling or flat, it looks endless
And droves of brown dogies are no company
They only remind you you're friendless

By night I can gaze at the stars
We all know the stars never bore us
I warble my song and the steers moo along
And the coyotes bark a fine chorus

Some cowboys coddle their horses
They think it's the kind way to treat 'em
But I made up my mind it's worse than unkind
When you know you might have to eat 'em

I see lovely ladies in town
They look away quick when I pass 'em
I may not be tough but I'm dirty and rough
And look like I'm apt to harass 'em

It's lonesome out here on the range
With only the cattle to sing to
No wonder by day, no comfort by night
And only my saddle to cling to

'L'

I love being 'L'
It's the one way to be
Such a wonder to hear
So amazing to see

Just look at an apple
Or listen to surf
How better prepare
To go under the turf?

The smile of your baby
Chestnuts in the park
The frown of your enemy
Bite of a shark

Feel sun after rain
And rain after drought
A frosty full moon
Fresh air in your mouth

So lovely to lie in
And cuddle your mate
And have a good session
And laugh at your fate

Lovely to get up
And fly like a kite
Work you believe in
Fight the good fight

The lance of a surgeon
The glance of a friend
Good food good drink
Days without end

It's great to be 'L'
Be brave be bold
And make up your mind
To live, and die old

My Neighbours' Windows
(Walking Song)

Walking by my neighbours' windows
Viewing what's on show
Blueing Christmas family photos
Taken years ago
Cheap Chinesee statuettes
What a lot of fuss
It makes you want to cry, the stuff
That means so much to us
Walking by my neighbours' windows
Seeing what's inside
Barbie dolls and Teddy bears
Exhibited with pride
Pampered-looking cats on silken
Cushions fast asleep
The things we treasure and preserve
They make you want to weep
Weep weep weep
They make you want to weep

Walking by my neighbours' windows
Spying them in there
Look away quickly, it's
Prohibited to stare
You might see naked bodies
That embrace us like a truss
Vile bodies we all cherish
They mean so much to us
Is that your neighbour's tackle?
Is that his hairy ruff?
Is that your neighbour's pelt or tassel?

Can you spot her muff?
We mustn't peep on neighbours
They may be in the buff
When you witness our sad bodies
You quickly see enough
When you see our naked bodies
Can you ever see enough?
When you see our naked bodies
You can never see enough
You can never see enough

No Room At The Inn (Carol)

No room at the inn
Tonight we have frost
Our babe nearly born
My wife needing rest

Sleeping in a barn
With her by my side
It's snug and it's warm
Pray God will provide

I feel the babe turn;
Rustling the straw
My wife gives a moan
And I am in awe

The three of us here
The Caesar's tax paid
And wonder of wonders
The child we have made

REFRAIN: Now sleeps the red rooster, now the white hen
The grey donkey shuffles and snores in his pen
They rest from labour; my wife's now begins
Our babe is ready; no room at the inn

Not Deleted Yet

Waiting for the doctor
She'll listen to my lungs
Say they're sounding better, not
Filling up with gunge

She'll say my heart is doing stuff
It shouldn't do at best
I'll smell of old Chanel—her button
Chilly on my chest

She'll twiddle her computer
While I fiddle with my clothes
Say I'm not deleted yet
From files God only knows

'O'

I hate being 'O'
Such a crap way to be
You can't see or hear
Takes forever to pee

Neck like a chicken
Teeth coloured grunge
Knees like noodles
Schlong like a sponge

Your zipper's half-mast
Your face is a wreck
Invisible now
To the opposite sex

And if you're a woman
Even a wag
You give in to gravity
All the bits sag

Your wrinkles grow wild
Like weeds on a tip
And for whom the bell tolls
Rings out when you strip

Crap waiting your turn
Uncertainty's certain
Whang! goes a loved one
Gone for a burton

Crap being trapped
On the very top rung
So make up your mind
To jump, and die young

Philtrum

Why have poets neglected thee
And lovers seem so bored?
Is it the mystery of your mark
That means you are ignored?

In the gauzy morning light
The rim of her philtrum glows;
Satin lips her overbite
Beneath the legendary nose
And brow so white.

Say, what is a philtrum for?
Is it a mere sluice for snot?
Not when it's one you adore
Cover with kisses moist and hot
It must be more

Are they baffled, pass you by
To praise a pink, rosebud lip,
A swelling breast, sparkling eye
Not your lovely, curious dip?
I wonder why

Why have poets neglected thee
And lovers seem so bored?
Is it the mystery of your mark
That means you are ignored?

Rock On, Crimson Cavalier

CHORUS: Rock on, Crimson Cavalier
Steam on, Sierra Blue
Dream on, Golden Supernova
Dreams are always true

Crimson Cavalier, keep rocking
In the car park by the wild wood
Rock on, never stop

Walk on, girl with white Suzuki
Walk your curly catwalk sheepdog
Try hard not to gawp

Sierra Sapphire, keep on steaming
Windows shut and fogging over
Steam on, never stop

Bog off, man in black Range Rover
Standing stiffly in the lay-by
Eyes about to pop

Burnt-out Nova in the beech wood
Do you dream of dancing lovers?
Dream on, let 'em bop

Dream you're Golden Supernova
Do the Samba on the green
Dream on, and never stop

Short Way Home

CHORUS: We take the short way
                Always the short way
                We can't wait to get home
                We take the short way
                Always the short way
                We always take the short way home

Soon we'll be off to Paris
Seems the right thing to do
After a long cold dark winter
Not everyone got through

We'll climb the little mountain
Visit the Sacred Heart
Lunch at our favourite café, the one
Built by the royal tart

We'll sit and sip our cocktails
After we stroll for miles
Floating past are unknown faces
Telling their unknown tales

MIDDLE EIGHT: It's great to go to Paris
                       Londontown or Rome
                       Berlin or Barcelona
                       But we take the short way home

We'll shop on the little island
Maybe find something chic
Browse the giant bookstore, the one
We'd like to browse all week

We'll see some famous pictures
Gaze at the golden dome
Say goodbye to cons and tricksters
Then take the short way home

The Speaker And The Mumbler (March)

The motivational speaker
His stroll is like a march
His smile like a dress parade
Uniform stiff with starch

The mumbler on his lonely bench
Cradles his lager can
He mutters a lot but few can hear
And no one understands

Will the speaker stop and listen?
Or have a word in his ear
When he's in the bushes pissing?
None will think it queer—
A talk on positive thinking
While he drains superfluous beer

No, the speaker stomps right on past
The mumbler mumbles on
One prefers an audience coming
The other an audience gone

Is all they have in common this common,
This patch of grassy hill?
Can't they talk about Death and Taxes?
The Triumph of the Will?

The Speaker and the Mumbler,
One hooked on drunk defeat,
The other on winning and winning and winning,
Who can't bear to be beat

Thriving Song

The alder tree has a mighty thirst
The cyclamen flower braves the frost
Foxgloves flourish on mud and dust
Cygnets travel wherever they must
We thrive where we belong, and we
Belong here together
Belong here together
Belong here together like butter on toast

The catwalk model needs his rags
The terrible tanker needs her tugs
Toddlers need their kisses and hugs
Does anyone need these glamorous wags?
We thrive on things we need, and we
Need to be together
Need to be together
Need to be together like hoovers and rugs

The partisan loves his trusty gun
The parakeet loves its crusty bun
The poetess loves her dusty pun
The parish priest loves that busty nun
We thrive on what we love, and we
Love to be together
Love to be together
Love to be together like tonic and gin

Tiger Bay: The Alternative Tour (Reggae)

O our Tiger Bay
We love Tiger Bay
Let 'em change her name
She won't be ashamed
Of her youth so fast
Of her dubious past
She will always be our Tiger Bay
We will always love our Tiger Bay

Here's a bronze of Ivor Novello
And his songs, romantic and mellow
Not dead on the page
He sings on the stage
Of the musical armadillo

Here's a church made of Norwegian wood
With a Welsh roof to shelter The Good
Captain Scott nearby
Continues to die
With his men, like a real captain should

Here's a bank that's still serving money
Not pina coladas with honey
Go on, order cash
They'll top up your stash
Or say no, are you being funny?

Here's a Nissen hut, stylish but bleak
What a shame there's no name—it's unique
It won a big prize
For architect guys
Who design sewage pumping with chic

Here's a fountain they call The Flourish
Both body and soul it can nourish
Have tea and a tart
And shop for some art—
Feel free—have a pee, flush and flourish

O our Tiger Bay
We love Tiger Bay
Let 'em change her name
She won't be ashamed
Of her youth so fast
Of her dubious past
She will always be our Tiger Bay
We will always love our Tiger Bay

Wake A Little Lust (Quick Waltz)

CHORUS:
Wake a little lust
Make a little trust
Shake it all about
Bake it in the oven
When you take it out
You got a lotta lovin'

Wrapped up in a towel
Fastened with a peg
Warm and damp and fluffy like
She's hatched from an egg
Something stirs inside him
Somewhere near the groin
Her peg calls his little peg
Unfasten and be mine!

Struggling with her suitcase
Broken lock today
Inanimate things always work
To spoil your holiday
Bending over naked
Showing her his back
Trying to fix the latch he feels
A hand caress his cheek

Sitting on the porch
Waiting for her man
Never sure when he'll turn up
He will when he can
Little flakes of trust

Falling from her heart
What he says and what he does
Can be so far apart

Lying on the beach
Topping up her tan
Bikini-roasted flesh the same
Colour as the sand
Once the sight of her
Moved him in the bone
Now he asks and she replies
As if she's made of stone

Standing on the kerb
Pizza slice in hand
Having a Nothing Moment while
His brain stops to scan
Pictures from the past
Copy to his heart
All the times he trusted her
Tell him she was right

Lounging in the garden
He watches people smoke
Coffee steaming at his elbow
Peaceful as the oak
She glides round the corner
Thumbs her nose and grins
Sticks her tongue out, starts the banter
Now the fun begins

Wedding Bell Blues (Klezmer Song)

CHORUS: Wedding bell blues
Wedding bell blues
When you got it all
You got it all to lose
Don't stop and worry
Keep moving your shoes
Dance away the wedding bell blues

Solomon and Sheba had wedding bell blues
They had a lot to give and had a lot to lose
They might have lost it all if they hadn't been true
But Solomon was wise and Sheba was too
And when they said 'I love you' there wasn't no schmooze
They danced away the wedding bell blues

Anthony and Cleo had wedding bell blues
They had a lot to give and had a lot to lose
They might have had each other and the Valley of the Nile
But wanted all the world and wanted it in style
They gambled all for love; the Romans turned the screws
And they lost it to the wedding bell blues

Darcy and Elizabeth had wedding bell blues
They had a lot to give and had a lot to lose
Lizzie had her pride but she loved him tenderly
Darcy loved her back but was Lord of Pemberley
Finally they kissed and started moving their shoes
And danced away the wedding bell blues

Mickey Mouse and Minnie have wedding bell blues
They have a lot to give and have a lot to lose
Fiances forever they've been courting so long
And never got married and you wonder what's wrong
They need a klezmer band and lots and lots of booze
To dance away the wedding bell blues

Little Ken and Barbie have wedding bell blues
They have a lot to give and have a lot to lose
Only made of plastic they have to use their wits
They've loads of accessories but no naughty bits
Their story's up to you; it's up to you to choose
What they do with the wedding bell blues

White Plastic Chair

CHORUS: O the white plastic chair
           It will always be there
           When they dig us up, monument and steeple,
           Millennia from now
           Prepare to take a bow
           We'll be renowned as The Plastic Chair People

When politicians meet
They stand up on their feet
And talk about a world that's right and fair
But before the talking's done
The fighting has begun
To get their bottoms on the white plastic chair

When high-ups of the churches
Come down off their perches
Announce it's time for rich and poor to share
Where have they got their buns?
Why go to Sally Lunn's?
You can have them in a white plastic chair

When a judge holding court
Criminal or tort
Is sorting out the miseries of Job
You'll find him high in air
In a white plastic chair
That's slyly hidden underneath his robe

When a Lord of Fourth Estate
Finds another Watergate
He'll buy it if he's got a soul to sell
But why is it for sale?
It isn't Chippendale
It's plastic, white, and comes in green as well.

When professors will process
In medieval-modern dress
And dole out their degrees to those who pass
It's the white Professor's Chair
That's waiting way up there
The throne to fit the academic ass

In a desert far away
From the heartless human fray
Where I had space to think and time to spare
I met an ancient gypsy
Selling rum and Pepsi
And got tipsy in his white plastic chair

Acknowledgements

Thanks to the members of Edgeworks writing group for all their insights and encouragement: Jane Blank, Deborah Kay Davies, Claire Syder, Andrew Smith, Ruth Smith.

Thanks to my song-writing mentor, Adrian May.

Thanks again to my book designer, Richard Cox.

Acknowledgements are due the following magazines: Poetry New York, Roundyhouse, and to Parthian Books for their years of support.

'Carrickfergus' and 'Rock on, Crimson Cavalier' are reprinted from my 2005 collection The More Deceived: poems about love and lovers; 'Carrickfergus' is written to be sung to the Irish air of the same name.

'A Morning Song', 'Drinking Song', 'Drowning Song', and 'Hanging Song' are from my previous collection, 'Hats', assembled in the 1960s.

Thanks to Tom Waits for his songs 'The Long Way Home' and 'Take It With Me' which were the starting points for two of my songs, 'The Short Way Home' and 'Cheshire Cat Moon'.

Thanks again to Roger Ellis, who like Robbie Burns taught me not to try to distinguish between songs and poems.

Thanks to Carol and Nick Evans, Carol for her critical comment, Nick for his music.

Thanks again to my writing buddy, Sue Habeshaw.

Thanks to Colin Stephens for helping with access to Campion's Book of Ayres.

Thanks to the staff and students of Severn Road Centre, Cardiff, especially to my computer teacher, Judith Henry.

Thanks to Ceri Rowlands and the staff of Canton Library, Cardiff.

Finally thanks to my wife Deborah for her unstinting love and nurture, and for her ability to combine the supposedly incompatible roles of muse and critic.

PARTHIAN

Tattoo
on Crow
Street

Kate
Noakes

Washing
My Hair
With
Nettles

Emilia
Ivancu

Living in the
Delta

Landeg White

POETRY